Easy Crafts in **5** Steps

Easy Bead Crafts in 5 Steps

Enslow Elementary

an imprint of

Enslow Publishers, Inc.

40 Industrial Road
Box 398
Berkeley Heights, NJ 07922
USA

http://www.enslow.com

Note to Kids: The materials used in this book are suggestions. If you do not have an item, use something similar. Use any color material and paint that you wish. Use your imagination!

Safety Note: Be sure to ask for help from an adult, if needed, to complete these crafts.

Note to Teachers and Parents: Crafts are prepared using air-drying clay. Please follow package directions. Children may use color clay or they may paint using poster paint once clay is completely dry. The colors used in this book are suggestions. Children may use any color clay, cardboard, pencils, or paint they wish. Let them use their imaginations!

Enslow Elementary, an imprint of Enslow Publishers, Inc.
Enslow Elementary® is a registered trademark of Enslow Publishers, Inc.

Translated from the Spanish edition by Ian Grenzeback, edited by Jaime Ramírez-Castilla, of Strictly Spanish, LLC. Edited and produced by Enslow Publishers, Inc.

Library of Congress Cataloging-in-Publication Data

Llimós Plomer, Anna.
  [Cuentas de colores. English]
  Easy bead crafts in 5 steps / Anna Llimós.
      p. cm. — (Easy crafts in 5 steps)
  Summary: "Presents bead craft projects that can be made in 5 steps"—Provided by publisher.
  Includes bibliographical references and index.
  ISBN-13: 978-0-7660-3082-4
  ISBN-10: 0-7660-3082-2
  1. Beadwork—Juvenile literature. I. Title.
  TT860.L5313 2007
  745.58'2—dc22
                            2007002430

Originally published in Spanish under the title *Cuentas de colores*.
Copyright © 2005 PARRAMÓN EDICIONES, S.A., - World Rights.
Published by Parramón Ediciones, S.A., Barcelona, Spain.
Text and development of the exercises: Anna Llimós
Photographs: Nos & Soto

Printed in Spain

10 9 8 7 6 5 4 3 2 1

To Our Readers: We have done our best to make sure all Internet Addresses in this book were active and appropriate when we went to press. However, the author and the publishers have no control over and assume no liability for the material available on those Internet sites or on other Web sites they may link to. Any comments or suggestions can be sent by e-mail to comments@enslow.com or to the address on the back cover.

Every effort has been made to locate all copyright holders of material used in this book. If any errors or omissions have occurred, corrections will be made in future editions of this book.

Contents

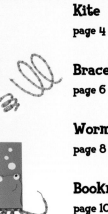

Kite

MATERIALS

Pencil
Construction paper
Plastic string
Wood beads
Clear tape
Scissors
Hole punch

1 Draw and cut a rhombus out of construction paper. Make a hole in one corner.

2 Thread a piece of plastic string through the hole and make a knot.

3 Cut out little squares and make a hole in the center of each one.

4 String three wood beads onto the string and then a square. Repeat this pattern, alternating colors.

5 Attach a piece of plastic string to the back of the kite with clear tape. You can use this to hang it up.

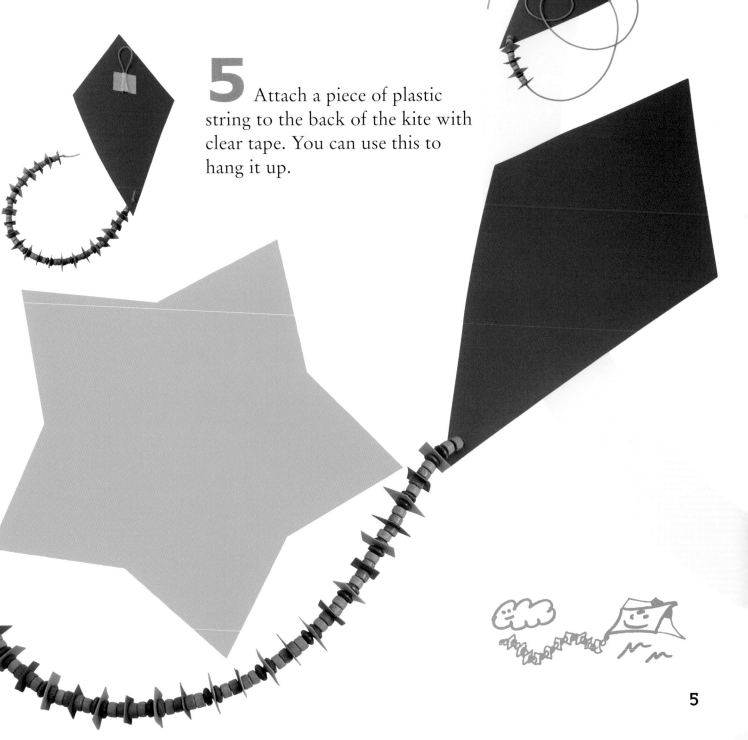

Bracelet and Ring

1 Ask an adult to help you bend over the end of a wire using pliers. String beads onto the wire.

MATERIALS

Plastic beads
Wire
Pliers

2 Keep on adding beads in the same order.

3 So the beads do not come off, bend the end over the same way you did before.

4 Wind the wire around your wrist to form a spiral.

5 Make a ring using a shorter piece of wire. Follow the same steps as for the bracelet.

Worm

MATERIALS

Air-drying clay
Crystal beads
Plastic beads
Tissue paper
Different colors of paint
Toothpicks or wooden skewers
Wire
Paintbrush
White glue
Pliers

1 Make some clay beads of different shapes and sizes. Put them on toothpicks or wooden skewers. Let dry.

2 Ask an adult to help you bend over the end of a wire using pliers. For the head, put a big, round clay bead onto the wire.

3 String on crystal, plastic, and clay beads until you reach the end of the wire.

4 Bend over the other end of the wire and paint the worm's face.

5 Twist the wire to get the worm into any position you like. Glue the tissue paper garland onto the worm's head.

Bookmark

Plastic beads
Poster board
Yarn
Marker
White glue
Scissors
Hole punch

1 Cut out a rectangle of poster board. Make four holes in one of the short sides.

2 Put a piece of yarn through one of the holes. String several beads onto it, and tie the ends.

3 Repeat step 2 with the three remaining holes to get eight octopus arms.

4 Draw the head of the octopus on poster board and cut it out.

5 Cut two eyes and three bubbles out of poster board. Glue them onto the rectangle. Paint the pupils and the mouth with a marker.

Wire House

MATERIALS

Red, orange, green, and
black wood beads
Wire
Pliers

1 Ask an adult to cut a piece of wire. Put seven red beads on it.

2 Put on ten orange beads, three green ones, twelve black ones, and three more green ones.

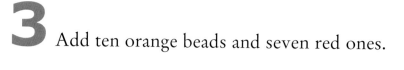

3 Add ten orange beads and seven red ones.

4 To make it into the shape of a house, bend the wire where the beads change color.

5 Ask an adult to bend over the ends of the wire using pliers. Fasten the ends together to close the shape of the house.

13

Clay NecKlace

MATERIALS

Air-drying clay
Plastic Knife
Different colors of paint
Thin rope
Toothpicks
Paintbrush
Scissors

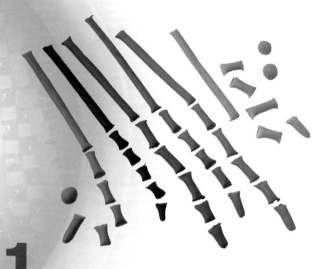

1 Make a roll of clay. Cut it into small, macaroni-shaped pieces. Make some balls for the clasps.

2 To make a hole in the beads, put the pieces on toothpicks.

3 Once the beads are dry, paint them any color.

4 String the beads on the thin rope.

5 To make the clasp, tie a ball onto one end of the string. Tie a slip knot at the other end.

Ballerina

MATERIALS

Small wood beads
Oval bead
Big button with two holes
Round bead
Different colors of paint
Thin rope
Paintbrush
Scissors

1 Make a knot in the middle of a thin rope. Put the two ends through the round bead (the head).

2 Tie another piece of thin rope below the head. Put beads on it for the arms. Knot the ends of the thin rope.

3 Pass the thin rope coming from the head through the oval bead to make the body.

16

4 String on the button to make the skirt.

5 Put some beads on the ends of the thin rope for the legs. Knot the ends. Paint eyes and a mouth on the head.

Peacock

MATERIALS

Plastic, wood, and
crystal beads
Air-drying clay
Wire
Pliers

1 Mold the body of the peacock out of clay. Make the beak and attach it to the body.

2 Ask an adult to help you bend over the end of a wire using pliers. Put two wood beads on it.

3 Put three plastic beads and one crystal bead on the wire. Repeat this pattern.

4 Repeat steps 2 and 3 until you have nine pieces total.

5 Stick the nine pieces of wire into the clay body of the peacock as the tail.

Star NecKlace

MATERIALS

Air-drying clay
Wood beads
Different colors of paint
Elastic string
Plastic knife
Round toothpick
Roller
Paintbrush

1 Flatten a piece of clay. Draw stars and trapezoids on it with a toothpick.

2 Cut the shapes out with a plastic knife. Put toothpicks through them to make holes.

3 Once they are dry, paint them.

20

4 String some wood beads onto a piece of elastic.

5 Put the clay trapezoids and stars in between. Tie the two ends of the elastic together when you finish.

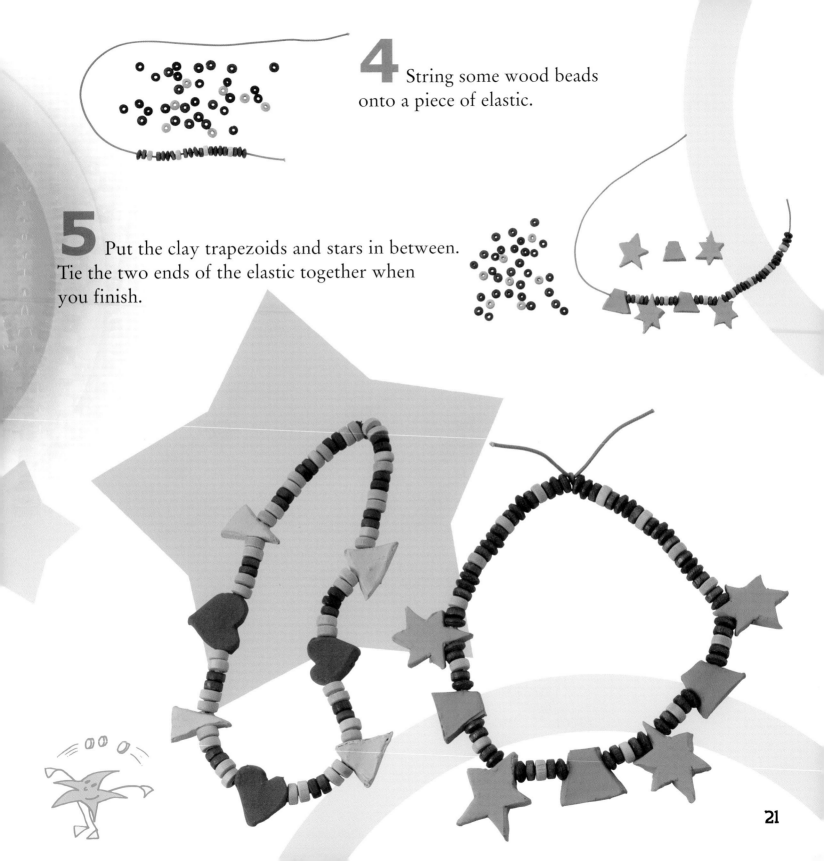

Flowers

MATERIALS

Wood beads
Flat beads
Elastic string
Scissors

1 Cut a piece of elastic string and tie off one end. String a wood bead onto it.

2 Add three flat beads and continue the pattern.

3 For the center of the flower, make a knot and tie on a bead of a different color.

4 Cut another piece of elastic string. String on some beads.

5 Tie the ends of the elastic to make a circle of petals. Fit it around the center of the flower.

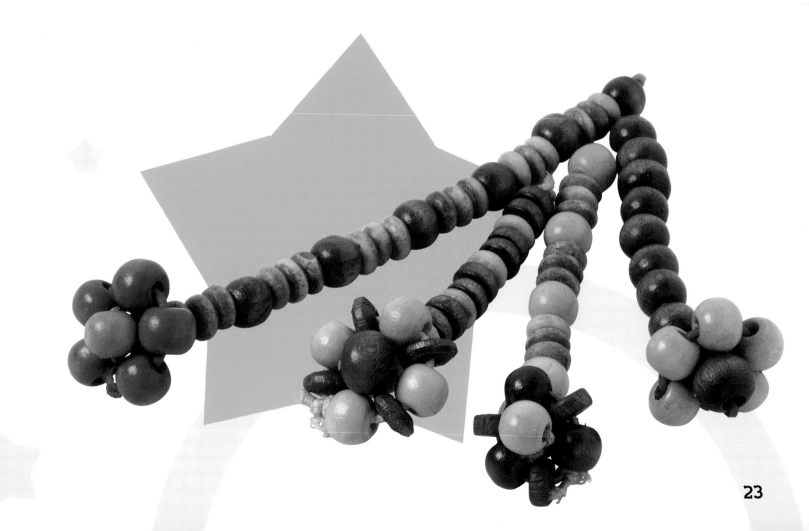

Necklace and Earrings

1 Cut pieces of flexible plastic tubes of different sizes.

MATERIALS

Plastic beads
Flexible plastic tubes
Metal headpins for the earrings
Earring hooks
Wire
Pliers
Scissors

2 Ask an adult to help you cut a piece of wire. Thread on the pieces of plastic tube and the plastic beads.

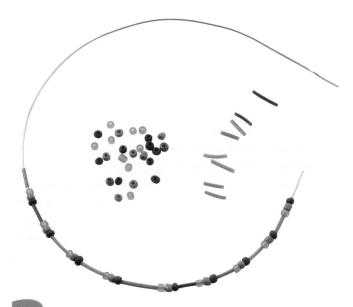

3 To make the clasp, put two longer flexible plastic tubes on the wire. Ask an adult to help you bend each end over with pliers.

4 Put some beads and a piece of plastic tube on the headpin for each earring.

5 To attach the hook, ask an adult to help you bend over the end of the wire with pliers.

Snake

1 Ask an adult to help you bend over the end of a piece of wire with pliers. Put one plastic bead and two wood beads on it.

2 Continue the pattern until you fill the whole wire. Bend over the end like you did in the first step.

3 To make the head, twist around one end of the wire.

26

4 Twist the wire in order to shape the body.

5 For the eyes, draw a black dot on two wood beads. Glue them onto the snake's head. Let dry.

Belt

MATERIALS

Wood beads
Different colors of thin rope
Scissors

1 Cut and tie off four pairs of thin rope.
Thread a bead onto each pair.

2 Thread on three beads so the four pairs are
fastened together.

3 Add four new beads.
Repeat the pattern.

4 Continue the pattern until you get a length long enough to use as a belt.

5 Braid each end of the thin rope. Tie it around your waist.

Napkin Ring

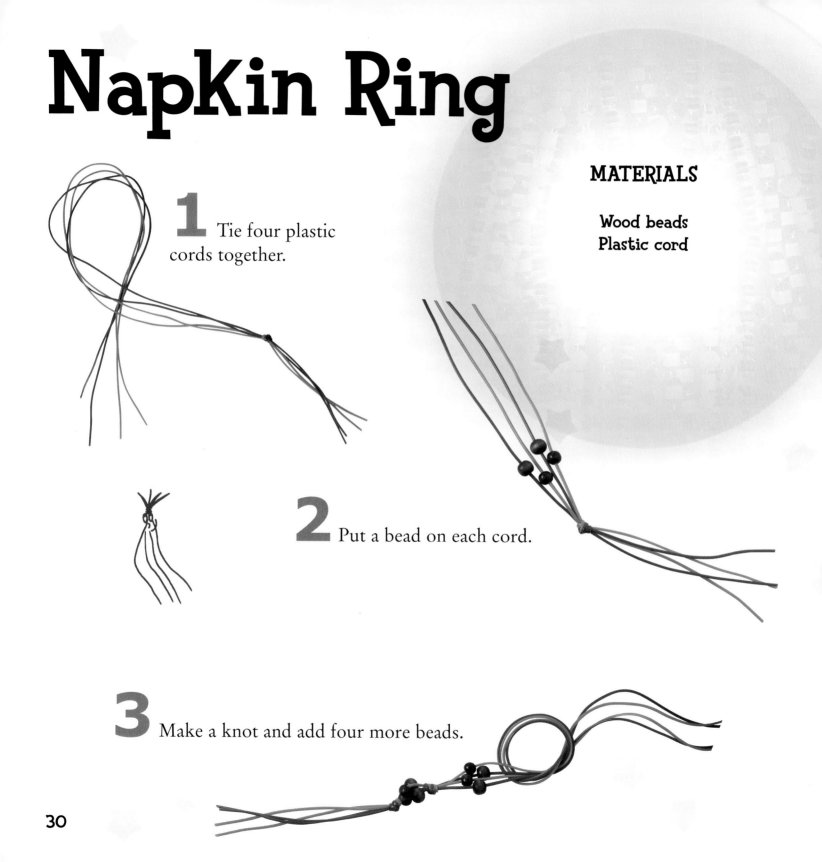

1 Tie four plastic cords together.

MATERIALS

Wood beads
Plastic cord

2 Put a bead on each cord.

3 Make a knot and add four more beads.

4 Continue the pattern. Once it is as long as you want, make a knot on each side.

5 Tie the two ends together and cut off the excess plastic cord.

Read About

Books

Ashfield, Ben. *Beading for Fun!* Minneapolis, Minn.: Compass Point Books, 2005.

Powell, Michelle. *Beadwork.* Chicago, Ill.: Heinemann, 2002.

Souter, Gillian. *Odds 'n' Ends Art.* Milwaukee, Wis.: Gareth Stevens Pub., 2002.

Internet Addresses

Crafts for Kids at Enchanted Learning
<http://www.enchantedlearning.com/crafts/>

Kids Craft Weekly
<http://www.kidscraftweekly.com/>

Index

Easy to Hard

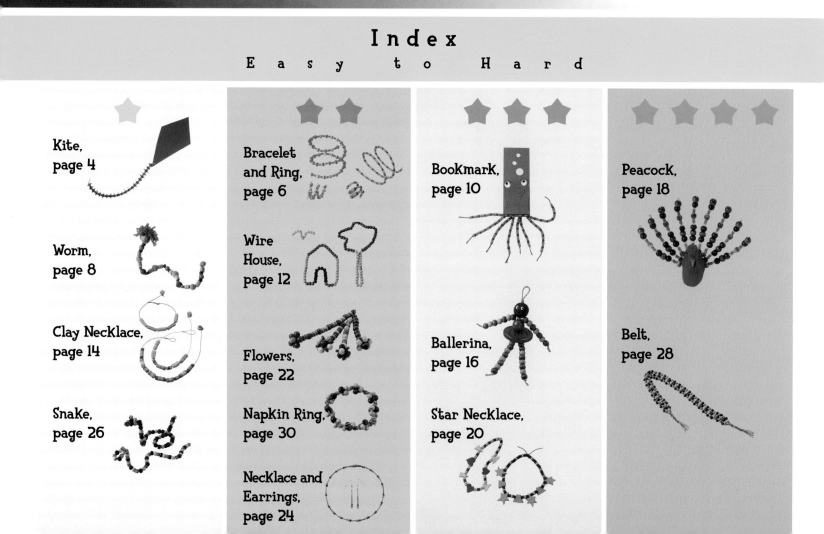